BEYND BLANKETS

WEAVING SUCCESSFUL BLANKET BUSINESS STRATEGIES FOR **2X GROWTH**

BEYOND BLANKETS

WEAVING SUCCESSFUL BLANKET BUSINESS STRATEGIES FOR 2X GROWTH

Sparsh Singla

Sarthak Singla

Worldwide Published by
Pendown Press

PENDOWN PRESS LLP

An ISO 9001 & ISO 14001 Certified Co.,

Regd. Office: 3767A, Kanhaiya Nagar,

Tri Nagar, Delhi-110035

Ph.: 8130886000, 9650072927

E-mail: info@pendownpress.com

Branch Office: 1A/2A, 20, Hari Sadan, Ansari Road,

Daryaganj, New Delhi-110002

Ph.: 011-45794768

Website: PendownPress.com

Edition: 2024

Price: ₹ 249

ISBN: 978-93-6338-479-8

Layout and Cover Designed by Pendown Graphics Team

Printed and Bound in India by Thomson Press India Ltd.

Contents

Acknowledgements

First and foremost, we would like to express our deepest gratitude to our parents, Mr. Kashmiri Singla and Mrs. Pooja Singla, whose wisdom, love, and guidance have shaped us into who we are today. We are eternally grateful for the strong foundation they have laid for us.

To my wife, Prapti Singla, your unwavering support and dedication have been the bedrock of everything I've accomplished. You have managed family responsibilities with grace, enabling me to focus on my work. I am truly blessed to have you by my side.

To my daughter, Kyrenne Singla, you are the true inspiration behind my journey. Your laughter, love, and dreams drive me every day to do better and be better. Sending all my love to you.

To our team at Jai Shree Radhey Texofab, it has been an honor to work alongside each of you. Your dedication, hard work, and belief in our vision have made this journey possible. We could not have achieved this without you.

To our customers, thank you for your trust and the insights you've shared with us over the years. Your experiences and feedback have been an invaluable source of inspiration for this book.

A heartfelt thank you to our dear friend, Mr. Dinesh Verma, CEO of Pendown Press, for your continuous support, guidance, and creative input throughout this process.

To the universe, for providing us with the strength, inspiration, and ideas needed to bring this book to life. Your support is felt in every word written.

And lastly, to all our loved ones—thank you for your unwavering encouragement, love, and support. Even if your names are not listed, you hold a special place in our hearts. This journey would not have been possible without you.

Preface

Hello, and welcome!

We're so glad you picked up this book, and we're confident that you'll find something here that truly resonates with you. This isn't just a collection of strategies or ideas; it's a conversation between us and you. Whether you're just starting your journey in the blanket business or have been in it for a while, this book is meant for everyone.

We believe that success isn't about following a one-size-fits-all formula. It's about understanding what works best for you, your customers, and your goals. That's why we've kept everything simple, practical, and grounded in real-life experiences. As you move through the chapters, think of this as a guide and a friendly chat with someone who's been there and done that. No complicated terms—just honest, straightforward advice on what really matters.

Throughout this book, you'll find insights that are easy to relate to, even if you've never run a business before. It's about learning from each other, sharing ideas, and finding better ways to grow together. From the basics to discovering how innovation can shape the future of your business, we'll walk with you through it all.

We want this to feel like you're getting advice from a trusted mentor who understands both the challenges and the victories you face. This is your book, your journey, and we're here to help guide you every step of the way.

Thank you for being part of this.

Why This Book?

Over the years, we've witnessed many of our brothers in the industry struggle due to challenges like lack of technology awareness, outdated methods, and not knowing where to begin. It's painful to watch talented individuals lose out because they're just not equipped with the right tools or knowledge. And that's exactly why we decided to write this book.

This book isn't just about us sharing what we know—it's about creating a bridge for others to succeed. We want to make sure that anyone, no matter where they are in their journey, has the chance to build something meaningful. Whether it's understanding the latest trends, overcoming common obstacles, or learning how to make smarter decisions, we've packed this book with everything we wish we had known earlier.

It's a guide that will help you grow, succeed, and make a mark in the blanket industry. We believe in the potential of every individual, and we want to see you rise and shine. This is our way of giving back, of supporting the industry we've spent so many years in, and of helping our brothers and sisters build a brighter, more successful future.

So, let's make it a fun and successful ride ahead!

CHAPTER 1

The Art and Science of Blankets

"Quality is not an act, it is a habit."

— Aristotle

A Brief History of Blankets and Their Evolution

Have you ever wondered how blankets became such an essential part of our lives? The journey began around 3000 BCE in Mesopotamia, where early weaving techniques emerged. Initially, our ancestors relied on animal skins for warmth, but as civilizations developed, so did the art of blanket-making. Ancient Egyptians crafted linen coverings, while the Greeks and Romans used woolen fabrics not only for warmth but also as symbols of status and prestige.

The Industrial Revolution in the 18th century marked a significant turning point in blanket production. Mass manufacturing made blankets more accessible and affordable, transforming them from luxury items into everyday essentials. This period also saw the introduction of new materials such as cotton and synthetic fibers, which further diversified blanket options.

India's Role as a Blanket Powerhouse

India is more than just a country of festivals and spices; it's also one of the largest blanket producers in the world. Why? It's simple:

a perfect blend of skilled artisans, high-quality raw materials, and modern manufacturing facilities.

Let's explore why India is such a big name when it comes to blankets.

1. **A Rich Heritage:** India's journey with textiles and blankets goes back centuries. Places like Kashmir are famous for their soft woolen blankets, while Gujarat and Rajasthan add vibrant handcrafted quilts to the mix. These traditional techniques, passed down through generations, give Indian blankets a unique charm and quality.

2. **Panipat:** The Blanket Hub: Panipat, known as the "City of Weavers," is the heart of India's blanket production. It's not just a local center; it's a global hub that supplies blankets to countries around the world. With its mix of skilled workers and advanced factories, Panipat plays a major role in keeping India at the top of the industry.

3. **Affordable Quality:** One of India's biggest strengths is its ability to make high-quality blankets at affordable prices. Thanks to a combination of skilled labor, locally available materials, and efficient manufacturing, Indian blankets offer great value for money.

4. **Global Reach:** Indian blankets are shipped to countries across Europe, Africa, the Middle East, and the Americas. People love these blankets for their durability, softness, and affordability. India's ability to cater to different tastes and needs makes it a favorite in international markets.

5. **Innovation in Production:** India isn't just about tradition—it's also about innovation. Factories here use advanced technologies like automated weaving and sustainable processes to stay ahead. From blankets made with recycled

materials to lightweight designs perfect for all climates, Indian manufacturers are constantly improving.

6. **Support from the Government:** Government initiatives like "Make in India" have given the textile industry a boost. Export policies and financial incentives help manufacturers improve their technology and expand their businesses, making India an even bigger player in the global market.

7. **Sustainability Matters:** With more people wanting eco-friendly products, Indian companies have stepped up. Many now produce blankets using organic cotton, bamboo fibers, and even recycled plastic bottles. These sustainable efforts not only help the environment but also attract buyers looking for responsible products.

The Bigger Picture

India's role in the global blanket market is built on tradition, innovation, and adaptability. As India continues to grow as a blanket powerhouse, it's clear there are endless opportunities for anyone looking to be part of this thriving industry.

Innovations That Changed the Industry

When you think of innovations in blankets, you might wonder, "What's there to innovate?" A lot, actually!

Let's start with materials. Gone are the days of relying solely on wool or cotton. Today, we have materials like fleece, microfiber, and blends that are softer, more durable, and easier to maintain. Then comes technology: think heated blankets with temperature controls or weighted blankets designed to reduce anxiety.

Sustainability is another game-changer. With the global focus on eco-friendly products, many companies now use recycled materials or natural dyes to create environmentally conscious options.

Even production methods have seen drastic changes. Automated looms, laser-cutting technologies, and digital designs make the process faster and more precise. These advancements have made high-quality blankets affordable for everyone while offering endless design possibilities.

Conclusion

Blankets may seem like a simple product, but they carry a rich history and a bright future. From ancient animal hides to today's tech-savvy options, the blanket industry has come a long way. With India playing a pivotal role and innovations driving the market, there's no limit to what's next.

Stay tuned—this is just the beginning of your journey to mastering the art and science of blankets!

CHAPTER 2

The Legacy of Excellence: 40 Years of Textile Mastery

"Do not wait to strike till the iron is hot,
but make it hot by striking."

— William Butler Yeats

Rooted in Tradition, Driven by Innovation

For over 40 years, we've been weaving dreams into reality, proving that with passion and persistence, every thread tells a story of success.

The Journey of a Textile Leader

In the 1980s, five brothers from a humble family in a small town began their journey in the textile industry, starting with yarn spinning. Their passion and commitment to excellence led them to set up a blanket manufacturing unit, which laid the foundation for what would become **Jai Shree Radhey Texo Fab.**

Over the years, fueled by their strong focus on quality and innovation, the business expanded and diversified its offerings. By 2014, **Jai Shree Radhey Texo Fab** had become a leader in the domestic textile market, with a growing presence overseas. Committed to exceeding customer expectations, the company continued to innovate and explore new territories, earning a reputation for quality both domestically and globally. Today, we are present in more than 8 countries and continue to expand our reach.

For over four decades, our company has stood as a leading force in the B2B textile sector, consistently aiming for perfection in every aspect of our operations. Our journey began with a firm dedication to delivering nothing short of excellence, a commitment that continues to drive us forward today.

Our relentless pursuit of excellence has placed us to the forefront of the industry, enabling us to serve as a reliable partner for enterprises seeking top-notch textiles. We take pride in surpassing customer expectations by offering a diverse range of premium-quality fabrics that not only prioritize comfort but also elevate style and functionality to new heights.

Milestones and Major Achievements

Our commitment to innovation, sustainability, and customer satisfaction has driven us to constantly push the boundaries of the industry and exceed expectations.

"In our journey of 40 years, we've achieved remarkable milestones—building state-of-the-art blanket factories, earning

the trust of over 200 loyal clients, empowering more than 1,500 dedicated employees, and expanding our reach to 8+ countries. Each milestone reflects our unwavering dedication to quality, innovation, and a vision to keep the world warm, one blanket at a time."

Major achievements:

"Rising from humble beginnings, we have achieved extraordinary milestones in record time. Our journey is marked by:"

➢ Operating 4 state-of-the-art factories

➢ Spanning over 20 acres of land dedicated to excellence in production

➢ Establishing ourselves as pioneers with our trusted brand, OCOZY

➢ Expanding into 8+ international markets with a focus on quality and innovation

Expertise

4 Reasons to Work with Jai Shree Radhey Texo Fab

Experience textile excellence with **JSR Texo Fab:** Trusted for superior quality, global reach, customizable solutions, and unmatched customer satisfaction.

1. **Personal Customer Attention:** Your satisfaction is our priority, and we're here to cater to your unique needs with attentive service and tailored solutions.

2. **Customizations Available:** Explore our customization options for bespoke designs and personalized touches, elevating your brand with unique and distinctive offerings.

3. **Ever-Evolving Designs:** Step into a world of timeless elegance and modern sophistication with our ever-evolving designs.

4. **Bulk Orders:** 500-5,000 Pieces Delivering quality bulk orders from 500 to 5,000 pieces with precision and efficiency, even within record time.

Vision and Values That Shaped Our Success

Trust, Quality & Excellence: GUARANTEED!

➢ **Vision:** Our vision extends beyond mere production; it covers every step of the product development process. From sourcing the finest raw materials to implementing strict quality control measures, we leave no stone unturned in our search for perfection. We believe that by prioritizing quality over quantity, we can not only meet but exceed the expectations of our customers worldwide.

➢ **Mission:** Rooted in India's rich heritage of textiles and manufacturing expertise, we envision a future where excellence is not just a goal, but a standard embedded in every fiber we produce. Our mission is to embrace innovation at every stage, invest in cutting-edge technology, and continuously nurture the talents of our team to push boundaries. Through this approach, we aim to redefine the very essence of Indian textile manufacturing and elevate it to new global standards.

➢ **Our Values:** Our reputation for quality excellence speaks for itself, and we remain committed to delivering superior textile products that ensure the satisfaction and loyalty of our customers. Our innovative mindset and adaptability keep us ahead of industry trends, offering cutting-edge solutions that evolve with customer needs. With a strong global reputation and strategic partnerships, we expand into international markets, building long-lasting relationships through customer-focused approaches and ethical practices. Our wide range of products serves multiple industries, making us the preferred choice for all home textile needs.

Why Choose Us? What Makes Us Stand Out

Unlocking Excellence: Why We're Your Ultimate Textile Partner

1. **Unmatched Quality Assurance:** We set the bar for excellence, making sure that every product goes through thorough quality checks to ensure durability and top-notch quality. This dedication builds trust with every purchase.

2. **Reliable and Timely Delivery:** We guarantee fast and efficient delivery, making sure your orders arrive on time. By consistently meeting customer expectations, we help build satisfaction and loyalty.

3. **Exceptional Customer Satisfaction:** Your needs come first. We ensure that every interaction goes beyond expectations. From quick responses to personalized help, we are committed to offering a smooth experience that leaves you happy every step of the way.

We may deal in textiles, but the real fabric of our success is hard work, passion, and the drive to keep moving forward!.

CHAPTER 3

Custom Solutions for Every Need

"Innovation distinguishes between a
leader and a follower."

– Steve Jobs

In the blanket business, no two customers are the same. Customers have different needs, preferences, and styles, and that's where customization becomes a game-changer. Let's dive into how customization shapes the industry.

Overview of Over 900 Blanket Types

Did you know there are more than 900 types of blankets in the market today? From luxurious fleece blankets to practical hospital bedding, the variety is incredible. Each type serves a unique purpose, whether it's for warmth, comfort, or even decorative appeal.

In India alone, the demand ranges from heavy wool blankets for colder regions to lightweight cotton ones for summer. Then there are niche options like travel blankets, baby blankets, or even yoga blankets. The more you understand these categories, the better you can match the right product with the right customer.

This vast variety also opens doors for businesses to cater to specific markets. For instance, hotels often look for bulk orders of durable yet soft blankets, while high-end customers might seek premium options with unique designs.

Tailoring Products to Customer Specifications

Customization isn't just about adding a logo or choosing a color—it's about understanding what your customers truly need. For example:

➢ A retailer might request blankets in non-standard sizes to suit specific furniture.

➢ A hotel chain may prefer blankets in particular colors to match their branding.

➢ Individual customers might ask for hypoallergenic materials or reversible designs for added convenience.

By listening carefully to these needs, you can create products that feel personal and special. This not only satisfies customers but also builds trust and enhances your reputation as a business that goes the extra mile.

Customization also adds value to your products. When customers feel they're getting exactly what they need, they're often willing to pay a premium, which boosts your profit margins.

Success Stories: Customization in Action

Let's look at some real examples of how customization has worked wonders.

> Take the example of a small blanket company that started offering personalized baby blankets. By allowing parents to choose colors and add names or birth dates, they quickly gained popularity among new parents looking for unique gifts. This simple customization option not only boosted sales but also created a loyal customer base that returned for future purchases as families grew.

> Another inspiring story comes from a company that specializes in corporate gifting. They began offering customized blankets featuring company logos or branding messages for corporate clients. This not only provided a practical gift option but also helped businesses strengthen their brand identity among employees and clients alike.

> An exporter tapped into international markets by adapting blanket designs to local preferences. For example, minimalistic designs worked well in Europe, while bold patterns found success in Middle Eastern markets. Understanding what customers valued helped the brand gain a foothold globally.

These stories showcase the power of tailoring products to customer needs. It's not just about selling—it's about showing customers you care enough to create something just for them.

Conclusion

Customization is the future of the blanket industry. It allows us to move beyond mass production and focus on creating value for every customer. By understanding their unique needs and offering personalized solutions, we can build stronger connections and grow our business.

⊘ ⊘ ⊘ ⊘

CHAPTER 4

Accelerating Your Business

**"Success is the sum of small efforts,
repeated day in and day out."**

– Robert Collier

In today's fast-paced market, success isn't just about making great products—it's about getting those products to the right people, quickly and efficiently. Whether you're a retailer, manufacturer, or distributor, finding ways to accelerate your business is crucial. Let's explore some effective strategies to speed up your growth while maintaining quality and expanding your reach.

Strategies for Balancing Quality with Quantity

One of the biggest challenges in the blanket industry is finding the right balance between quality and quantity. You want to produce enough to meet demand, but you also don't want to compromise on the standard of your product.

Here's how you can strike that balance:

➢ **Focus on Efficient Production:** Streamline your processes to increase production capacity without sacrificing quality. For example, using automated stitching machines can speed up the production process while maintaining consistency.

➢ **Use Quality Materials in Bulk:** Buying high-quality materials in larger quantities can reduce costs and ensure the products stay premium. Just make sure the raw materials you source meet your standards and can be used across multiple product lines.

➢ **Start Small, Scale Up:** Begin with a smaller batch for new designs or collections. This allows you to test the market while ensuring your quality remains intact. Once you know it's a hit, scale up production with the confidence that the demand is there.

Balancing quality and quantity isn't easy, but with the right approach, you can grow your business without losing what makes your products special.

Streamlining Operations for Faster Delivery

Speed matters—especially in a market that values quick delivery. Customers expect fast service, and businesses that can't meet these demands risk losing their edge. Here's how to speed up your operations:

➢ **Optimize Your Supply Chain:** Look for ways to reduce delays in getting raw materials. Building good relationships with trusted suppliers can help ensure you get the right materials at the right time.

➢ **Implement Lean Practices:** Avoid waste in your processes. By focusing on lean manufacturing, you can minimize unnecessary steps, reduce costs, and speed up production.

➢ **Use Technology for Tracking:** Keep track of orders and inventory in real time. By using software to manage stock and shipments, you can respond faster to changes in demand and ensure quicker deliveries to your customers.

Faster delivery doesn't just keep your customers happy—it also gives you a competitive edge in a crowded market.

Effective Marketing to Maximize Reach

Even with the best products and streamlined operations, your business won't grow if no one knows about it. Marketing plays a huge role in expanding your reach and attracting new customers. Here are a few simple yet effective marketing strategies:

➢ **Use Social Media:** Social platforms like Instagram, Facebook, WhatsApp, etc. are great for showcasing your blankets. Share customer stories, behind-the-scenes content, and seasonal promotions to engage your audience.

➢ **Leverage Influencers:** Partner with influencers who align with your brand. They can help spread the word and bring your products to a wider audience.

➢ **Create Targeted Campaigns:** Focus on specific customer segments, such as families, hotels, or corporate clients. Tailor your marketing messages to address their unique needs, whether it's warmth for winter or eco-friendly options.

> **Build Your Online Presence:** Having a strong online presence is essential. Optimize your website, run paid ads, and ensure your online store is user-friendly. The easier it is for customers to shop, the more likely they are to buy.

With the right marketing strategies, you can get your brand in front of more people and accelerate growth in no time.

Conclusion

To accelerate your business, it's essential to find a balance between quality and quantity, streamline your operations, and use effective marketing to reach more customers. With these strategies, you can grow faster without compromising on what makes your products stand out.

CHAPTER 5

Overcoming Challenges Hand in Hand

"Alone we can do so little; together we can do so much."

– Helen Keller

Every business faces challenges, and the blanket industry is no different. But here's the good part: when we work together, learn from each other, and share our ideas, we can solve even the toughest problems. Let's explore this further.

Identifying Common Ground and Finding Unique Solutions

In the blanket business, we all face some common hurdles—fluctuating demand, changing customer preferences, rising costs, or even supply chain delays. But have you noticed how different businesses tackle these problems in their unique ways?

The first step to solving challenges is finding common ground. What's affecting everyone? Is it the cost of raw materials, or maybe the lack of skilled workers? Once we know the main problems, we can start finding unique solutions that are different from the usual approaches.

For example, one manufacturer dealt with rising material costs by using recycled yarn. Another started offering seasonal designs to attract new customers. These innovative ideas don't just solve problems; they also set you apart from competitors.

These ideas don't just fix the problems—they also help businesses stand out. And when we share these solutions with each other, it helps everyone move forward.

Tips We've Learned Together for Selecting Superior Products

Choosing the right products is one of the biggest challenges in the blanket business. Whether you're a manufacturer, retailer, or wholesaler, making the wrong choice can lead to losses. Over time, we've learned a few things that can help.

1. **Understand Your Market:** Start by knowing what your customers want. Are they looking for luxury blankets, budget-friendly options, or something sustainable? The more you understand their preferences, the easier it is to choose products that sell.

2. **Test Before You Commit:** Before investing heavily in new designs or materials, test them in smaller batches. This way, you can check customer interest without taking big risks.

3. **Focus on Quality:** No matter how affordable or trendy a product is, customers always appreciate good quality. Look for durable fabrics, neat stitching, and a finish that feels premium.

4. **Keep an Eye on Trends:** Staying updated on global trends, like weighted blankets or eco-friendly options, can give you an edge.

These tips are simple but powerful, and they come from real experiences in the industry. When we share what we've learned, it benefits everyone.

Shared Experiences: Learning from Each Other

The best lessons often come from each other's stories. For example:

➤ A retailer shared how offering personalized blankets helped them build strong relationships with customers.

➤ A manufacturer explained how they saved money by reducing waste during production.

Hearing such experiences helps us avoid common mistakes and discover new ideas.

Learning from others doesn't just save time—it also helps avoid common mistakes. For instance, one distributor found out that overstocking seasonal designs caused losses, so they now plan their inventory carefully.

Sharing these stories doesn't just help us grow; it also builds a sense of community.

We're not just competitors; we're part of a bigger network, helping each other grow.

Conclusion

Challenges are easier to overcome when we work together. By identifying problems, sharing tips, and learning from each other, we can solve issues and grow stronger.

CHAPTER 6

Looking Ahead:
The Future of Blankets

"The future depends on what we do in the present."

– Mahatma Gandhi

The blanket industry has come a long way, but the journey doesn't stop here. With new innovations and shifting consumer demands, the future looks bright. As we look ahead, it's important to keep an eye on emerging trends, technological advancements, and India's growing influence in the global market. This chapter will explore what's next for the blanket industry and how we can stay ahead of the curve.

Emerging Trends in Design and Technology

➢ **Sustainable and Eco-Friendly Fabrics:** One of the biggest trends is the increasing demand for sustainable, eco-friendly materials. Consumers are becoming more conscious of the environment, and businesses are responding by using recycled fabrics, organic cotton, and bamboo fibers. These materials not only help reduce our carbon footprint but also appeal to eco-conscious buyers.

➢ **Smart Blankets:** Technology is starting to find its way into blankets too. Smart blankets equipped with heating and cooling systems are becoming popular, allowing users to adjust the temperature to their liking. Some blankets even have built-in sensors that monitor sleep patterns and offer personalized comfort.

➢ **Textured and Multi-Functional Designs:** People now want blankets that do more than just keep them warm. Blankets with pockets, weighted features, or ones that can be used as throws or pillows are becoming popular. These designs are great for those looking for extra convenience and flexibility.

As trends evolve, businesses must adapt quickly to stay competitive, offering products that cater to changing preferences.

How Technological Innovations Enhance Production

Technology is not only changing the way we design blankets; it's also revolutionizing how they're produced.

➢ **Automation and Robotics:** Automated machinery and robotics are becoming more common in blanket production. These innovations help speed up manufacturing, reduce human error, and maintain consistency across large batches.

➢ **3D Knitting and Weaving:** Advances in 3D knitting technology allow manufacturers to create blankets with intricate patterns and textures, giving customers more variety and customization options.

➢ **Artificial Intelligence for Quality Control:** AI-powered systems are now being used to monitor production lines in real-time, ensuring high quality and identifying defects early. This helps reduce waste, improve efficiency, and maintain product quality across large-scale production.

➢ **Advanced Fabric Printing:** With digital printing technology, manufacturers can now print custom designs directly onto fabrics with incredible precision and detail. This has made it easier to offer a wider variety of colors, patterns, and styles in a shorter amount of time.

By embracing technological innovations, manufacturers can streamline production, reduce costs, and meet growing demand more effectively.

Predicting India's Growing Influence

India has always been a major player in the blanket industry, but its influence is only set to grow in the coming years.

➢ **Manufacturing Powerhouse:** As the demand for blankets continues to rise globally, India's manufacturing capacity is expected to expand even further, solidifying its position as a key player in the industry.

➢ **Export Growth:** With the rise of e-commerce and improved logistics, Indian blanket manufacturers are tapping into international markets like never before. Exporting to countries across Europe, the Middle East, and the U.S. is becoming increasingly easier, and this trend is expected to continue.

> **Affordable Innovation:** India's ability to combine quality with affordability is setting it apart. The country's manufacturing expertise allows it to produce high-quality products at competitive prices, which is attracting a growing number of international customers.

> **Rising Domestic Demand:** As the domestic market continues to expand, India's middle class is expected to drive growth in blanket sales. Increasing awareness of comfort and lifestyle products is pushing Indian consumers to seek better quality and more innovative options, creating new opportunities for manufacturers.

India's influence on the blanket industry will only continue to increase, making it an exciting time for businesses in the country to expand their reach both locally and globally.

Conclusion

The future of the blanket industry is filled with exciting possibilities. From innovative designs and smart fabrics to advancements in production technology, there's no doubt that the industry will keep evolving. India's growing influence on the global stage is another trend to watch, offering endless opportunities for growth and expansion.

Conclusion

A Recap of Our Shared Path

As we look back on this journey, it's clear how far we've come. From exploring the history of blankets to diving into innovative solutions, each step has been a milestone in shaping a future filled with endless possibilities. Along the way, we've shared experiences, tackled challenges, and embraced new ideas—all while focusing on what truly matters: delivering quality products that make a difference.

The industry's growth, the rise of customization, and the advancements in technology are just a few of the exciting changes we've seen. Together, we've witnessed how adapting to trends, investing in innovation, and staying connected with customer needs can set the stage for success. Each chapter we've covered has added a new layer to the bigger picture, reminding us that *growth is not just about numbers; it's about the people, the ideas, and the shared journey.*

Next Steps to Our Continued Success

The path ahead is bright. With the insights and strategies we've explored, there's no limit to what we can achieve together. As we move forward, here are a few key steps to keep in mind:

➢ **Keep Innovating:** Embrace the trends and technologies that shape the future. Whether it's smart blankets, sustainable fabrics, or streamlined production methods, staying ahead of the curve will keep us relevant and competitive.

➢ **Focus on Customer Experience:** Continue building strong relationships with our customers by offering personalized solutions, keeping them at the heart of everything we do.

Together, we've built a foundation of success. Now, it's time to take everything we've learned and make our mark on the future. The next chapter of our journey is full of new opportunities—let's seize them and keep moving.

A Thank You Note to Our Readers and Partners

Thank you for being a part of this journey. Whether you're a reader seeking inspiration or a partner working side by side with us, your support has been invaluable. We've come a long way together, and it's because of your trust and dedication that we're able to share these insights and strategies with you.

As we continue to grow and innovate, we invite you to stay connected and engage with us. If you're looking for further collaboration, have any questions, or simply want to share your thoughts, feel free to reach out! We believe that the best ideas come from open conversations, and we'd love to hear from you.

Let's Connect

Email: sparsh@jsrtexofab.com, sarthak@jsrtexofab.com

Contact Number: +91-9996699000, +91-9992254321

Address: Panipat, Haryana, India

We look forward to collaborating with you, learning from each other, and growing together. Thank you for being an essential part of our community.

⊘ ⊘ ⊘ ⊘

Frequently Asked Questions

We've gathered some of the most common questions from our customers, and we've provided answers to help clarify and guide you on your journey. If you have any additional questions, don't hesitate to reach out to us!

Q.1   What sets your blankets apart from others in the market?

Ans. Our blankets stand out due to the combination of high-quality materials, innovative designs, and customization options. We focus on comfort, durability, and ensuring that each product meets our customers' specific needs.

Q.2   How do I get started with a custom order?

Ans. Getting started is easy! Simply reach out to us through email or our contact form, and we'll guide you through the entire process, from selecting the right fabric to personalizing your design.

Q.3   Can I order in bulk for my business?

Ans. Absolutely! We offer bulk orders for businesses, ensuring that you get quality products at competitive rates.

Q.4   What's the typical turnaround time for custom orders?

Ans. Turnaround times vary depending on the complexity and quantity of your order. Generally, custom orders are completed within 10-15 business days, but we're always happy to provide more specific timelines upon inquiry.

Q.5 Do you offer sustainable options?

Ans. Yes, sustainability is a key priority for us. We offer a range of eco-friendly materials like organic cotton and recycled fabrics, ensuring that our products align with both comfort and environmental responsibility.

We hope these answers help, but if you have any other questions, we're just an email or phone call away. Let's keep the conversation going!